DAD DIED
NOW WHAT

An Educational Guide for Handling a Death

Wayne Cass

ISBN: 9798388192516
Design and Formatting by Keilah Cass

CONTENTS

LOSS

I'm sorry to hear about your loss. Losing a loved one is a difficult and emotional experience, and it's important to take care of yourself during this time. There are a few things you may need to do following the death of a loved one, including:

Inform family and friends: It's important to let close family and friends know about the death of your loved one as soon as possible. This can be done through phone calls, emails, or social media.

Contact the appropriate authorities: Depending on the circumstances of the death, you may need to contact the police, a coroner, or other authorities.

Arrange the funeral or memorial service: You will need to decide on the details of the funeral or memorial service, including the location, the type of service, and who will officiate.

Take care of practical matters: There may be a number of practical matters that need to be taken care of, such as cancelling credit cards and accounts, transferring ownership of assets, and making arrangements for the care of any dependents.

Seek support: It's important to take care of your own emotional well-being during this difficult time. Consider seeking support from friends, family, or a professional counselor.

It's understandable to feel overwhelmed by these tasks. It may be helpful to enlist the help of friends, family, or a professional to assist you in handling these responsibilities. Take your time and don't hesitate to ask for help when you need it.

COPING

Here are some steps you can take to help cope with this loss:

Offer support and comfort: Let your child know that you are there for them and that it is okay to feel a range of emotions, including sadness, anger, and confusion. Encourage them to talk about their feelings and offer a supportive ear.

Encourage them to seek additional support: It can be helpful to talk to a counselor or therapist about their grief. They may also find comfort in talking to other family members, friends, or a religious leader.

Help them understand the grieving process: It can be helpful to explain to your child that grief is a normal and natural reaction to loss. It is okay for them to experience a range of emotions and for the intensity of their feelings to come and go. It is also important to let them know that it is okay to take their time in grieving and that there is no "right" way to grieve.

Help them find ways to honor their loved one: Encourage your child to find ways to remember and honor their loved one, whether that be through creating a memorial, participating in a meaningful activity, or sharing memories with others.

Take care of yourself. It's important to remember that you also need support and care during this difficult time. Make sure to take care of your own emotional and physical wellbeing so that you can be there for your child.

Grief is a natural and normal reaction to loss, and it is a highly personal experience that varies from person to person. Some people may experience a wide range of emotions, while others may experience a more narrow range. The grieving process typically involves a series of stages or steps, including:

Shock and denial: In the immediate aftermath of a loss, it is common for people to feel numb and in disbelief. They may feel like they are in a state of shock and may have trouble accepting that the loss has occurred.

Pain and guilt: As the reality of the loss sinks in, people may experience a deep sense of pain and sadness. They may also feel guilty or blame themselves for the loss.

Anger and bargaining: People may feel angry at the person who has died, at themselves, or at the circumstances that led to the loss. They may also try to bargain with a higher power or make deals in an attempt to reverse the loss.

Depression: People may feel a sense of despair and hopelessness as they come to terms with the reality of the loss. They may also experience a loss of interest in activities that they used to enjoy.

Acceptance: Eventually, people may come to accept the reality of the loss and begin to move forward. This does not mean that they have "gotten over" the loss, but rather that they have learned to live with it and find ways to cope with their grief.

It is important to note that these stages are not necessarily linear and that people may experience them in a different order or may not experience all of them. The grieving process can be difficult and may take some time, but it is a necessary part of healing after a loss.

FINANCIAL CONSIDERATIONS

There are often a number of costs associated with their funeral and final arrangements. These can include:

Funeral home services: This can include the cost of transporting the body, preparing it for burial or cremation, and hosting a funeral service.

Burial or cremation: The cost of burying a body in a cemetery plot or cremating it can vary widely, depending on the location and the type of service chosen.

Headstone or grave marker: If a burial is chosen, the cost of a headstone or grave marker may also be a consideration.

Obituary: Some people choose to place an obituary in a local newspaper or online, which can also have a cost associated with it.

Other expenses: There may be other expenses associated with a death, such as the cost of a death certificate or the cost of transporting family members to the funeral.

It is important to be aware of these costs and to plan ahead if possible. Many funeral homes offer payment plans or accept life insurance policies as a form of payment. It can also be helpful to talk to a financial planner or estate attorney to understand the financial implications of a death in the family.

PLANNER CONSIDERATIONS

Choose financial planner or estate attorney.

A financial planner is a professional who helps individuals and families manage their financial affairs and make informed decisions about their money. Financial planners offer a wide range of services, including:

Developing a financial plan: A financial planner can help you create a customized plan that outlines your financial goals and provides strategies for achieving them. This may include creating a budget, saving for retirement, paying off debt, or saving for a major purchase or event.

Providing investment advice: Financial planners can help you develop a portfolio of investments that aligns with your financial goals and risk tolerance. They can also provide guidance on how to diversify your investments and manage risk. Be independent.

Offering retirement planning services: Financial planners can help you plan for retirement by assessing your current financial situation, projecting your future needs, and recommending strategies for accumulating and preserving wealth.

Providing tax planning services: Financial planners can help you understand the tax implications of your financial decisions and recommend strategies for minimizing your tax burden.

Assisting with estate planning: Financial planners can provide guidance on issues related to estate planning, such as creating a will or trust, choosing a guardian for minor children, and making provisions for end-of-life care.

Financial planners typically charge a fee for their services, which may be based on an hourly rate, a flat fee, or a percentage of assets under management. It is important to carefully consider the qualifications and experience of a financial planner before hiring one.

An estate attorney is a type of lawyer who specializes in helping individuals and families plan for the transfer of their assets after death. This can include drafting wills, trusts, and other documents to ensure that a person's assets are distributed according to their wishes. Estate attorneys can also help with the probate process, which is the legal process of administering a person's estate after they die. This can involve collecting and valuing the person's assets, paying their debts and taxes, and distributing the remaining assets to their heirs or beneficiaries. Estate attorneys can provide guidance on a wide range of issues related to estate planning and probate, including tax laws, real estate, and charitable giving.

SERVICE CONSIDERATIONS

There are many different types of funerals that exist, and the type of funeral that is chosen can depend on a variety of factors including cultural and religious traditions, personal preferences, and financial considerations. Some common types of funerals include:

Traditional funeral: This is the most common type of funeral and typically includes a viewing or visitation, a funeral service, and a burial. The body is typically present at the funeral and may be embalmed and placed in a casket.

Cremation: Instead of a burial, the body is cremated after the funeral. The cremated remains, also known as ashes, can be interred in a cemetery, scattered in a special place, or kept by the family. A funeral service with the cremated remains present can be held before or after the cremation.

Graveside service: A graveside service is a brief ceremony that takes place at the grave site. It may be held in conjunction with a traditional funeral or as a standalone service.

Green burial: A green burial is a way of returning the body to the earth in a natural and eco-friendly manner. The body is typically not embalmed and is buried in a biodegradable casket or shroud.

Home funeral: A home funeral is when the family takes on the responsibilities of caring for the body and arranging the funeral themselves, rather than using a funeral home. This can include preparing the body for viewing, arranging transportation to the cemetery, and handling the legal and administrative aspects of the funeral.

These are just a few examples of the types of funerals that exist. The choice of funeral will depend on the individual and their family's preferences and beliefs.

A memorial service is a celebration of the life of the deceased without the body present. The service may be held at a funeral home, a church, or another location and may include eulogies, music, and other elements to honor the person who has died. There are many different types of memorial services that can be held to honor the life of a loved one. Some common types of memorial services include:

Traditional memorial service: This is a formal ceremony that is held in a church or funeral home and includes elements such as eulogies, music, and readings. The body may or may not be present at the service.

Celebration of life: A celebration of life is a more informal memorial service that is meant to celebrate the life of the deceased. It may be held at a venue such as a park or community center and may include elements such as music, storytelling, and activities that reflect the interests and passions of the person who has died.

Scattering of ashes: This is a ceremony in which the cremated remains of the deceased are scattered in a special place that was significant to them. The ceremony may be held at the scattering site or at a separate location, and may include elements such as music, readings, and a brief eulogy.

Online memorial service: With the rise of technology, it is now possible to hold a memorial service online. This can be a good option for those who are unable to attend a traditional service in person due to distance or other reasons.

Private memorial service: A private memorial service is a small, intimate gathering of close family and friends to pay their respects to the deceased. It may be held at the family's home or at a small venue such as a chapel.

There are many other types of memorial services that can be tailored to the specific needs and preferences of the family and the deceased. The most important thing is to create a service that accurately reflects the life and personality of the person who has passed away and provides a sense of closure and comfort to those who are grieving.

ORGAN DONATION

Organ donation is the process of surgically removing organs or tissue from a living or deceased person and transplanting them into another person. Organ donation can be a life-saving procedure for individuals who are suffering from organ failure or other serious health conditions.

If you are interested in becoming an organ donor, you can indicate your wishes on your driver's license or state ID card, or by signing up on the organ donor registry in your state. You can also specify your organ donation wishes in a living will or other advance directive.

When a person becomes a potential organ donor, the organ procurement organization (OPO) in their area is notified. The OPO works with the hospital to determine whether the person is medically suitable to donate their organs. If the person is deemed a suitable donor, the OPO will coordinate the organ recovery process.

Organs that can be donated include the heart, lungs, liver, kidneys, pancreas, and small intestine. Tissue that can be donated includes corneas, skin, bone, and heart valves.

After the organs or tissue have been recovered, they are transported to the recipient hospital where the transplant surgery will be performed. The recipient is usually someone who is on a waiting list for a particular organ and is a match for the donor.

Organ donation is a complex and sensitive process that requires careful coordination and planning. It is important to discuss your wishes about organ donation with your family and healthcare provider so that they are aware of your decision in the event that you are unable to express your wishes at the time of your death.

BUDGET CONSIDERATIONS

A household budget is a financial plan that outlines how you will allocate your income and expenses over a certain period of time, usually a month. The purpose of a household budget is to help you manage your finances, save money, and reach your financial goals.

The amount you should budget for each category will depend on your individual circumstances, such as your income, debts, expenses, and financial goals. Here are some general guidelines to help you create a household budget:

Start by calculating your total monthly income from all sources, including salary, investments, and any other sources of income.

Make a list of all your fixed expenses, such as rent or mortgage payments, insurance premiums, and car payments.

Make a list of your variable expenses, such as groceries, utilities, entertainment, and subscriptions.

Subtract your total expenses from your total income to see if you have a surplus or deficit. If you have a surplus, you can use the extra money to pay off debt, save for the future, or invest in your goals. If you have a deficit, you may need to make some adjustments to your budget to bring your expenses in line with your income.

Review your budget regularly and make adjustments as needed. Your budget should be a living document that reflects your changing financial situation.

It's important to remember that every household is different, and what works for one family may not work for another. The key is to find a budget that works for you and your family, and to stick to it as closely as possible.

Here is an example of a household budget for a family with a monthly income of $5,000:

Income:

Salary: $4,500

Investment income: $500

Total income: $5,000

Expenses:

Rent or mortgage: $1,500

Utilities (electricity, gas, water): $200

Internet and phone: $100

Groceries: $400

Transportation (car payments, gas, insurance): $500

Entertainment (movies, dinners out, etc.): $200

Clothing: $100

Gifts and charitable giving: $100

Health and personal care (doctors' visits, medications): $200

Debt payments (credit card, student loans): $500

Savings (emergency fund, retirement): $500

Total expenses: $4,800

Surplus: $200

This budget shows that the family has a surplus of $200 per month. They can use this extra money to pay off debt, save for the future, or invest in their goals. However, it's important to note that this is just an example, and actual budgets will vary depending on individual circumstances and financial goals.

INSURANCE CONSIDERATIONS

There are several types of insurance that a person may want to consider, depending on their specific needs and circumstances. Some common types of insurance that a person may want to consider include:

Health insurance: This type of insurance helps cover the cost of medical care, including doctor's visits, hospital stays, and prescription medications.

Life insurance: This type of insurance provides financial protection for your loved ones in the event of your death.

Disability insurance: This type of insurance provides income protection if you are unable to work due to a disability.

Homeowners insurance: This type of insurance provides protection for your home and personal property in the event of damage or loss due to a covered event, such as a fire or theft.

Auto insurance: This type of insurance provides protection for your vehicle in the event of an accident or other covered event.

Renters insurance: This type of insurance provides protection for your personal property if you are renting a home or apartment.

It is important to carefully consider your specific needs and circumstances when deciding which types of insurance to purchase. You may want to consult with an insurance professional or financial advisor to help you determine the types of insurance that are right for you.

It is generally a good idea to review and update insurances periodically to ensure that it reflects a person's current circumstances.

Some common events that may prompt a person to update their insurances include:

Marriage or divorce: A person's insurance should be updated after they get married or divorced, as these events can significantly affect how their insurances are distributed.

Birth or adoption of a child: They may want to update their insurance to provide for the care of their child in the event of their death.

Changes in assets or beneficiaries: If a person acquires or disposes of significant assets, or if their intended beneficiaries

PENSION CONSIDERATIONS

A pension is a type of retirement savings plan that provides regular payments to individuals during their retirement years. Pensions are typically funded by an employer or a union, and the payments are based on the employee's salary and length of service with the organization.

There are several different types of pensions, including defined benefit plans and defined contribution plans. In a defined benefit plan, the employer guarantees a certain level of payment to the employee upon retirement, based on factors such as the employee's salary and length of service. In a defined contribution plan, the employer and employee both contribute to a retirement account, and the employee's benefits are based on the balance in the account at the time of retirement.

Whether or not you should get a pension depends on your individual circumstances and retirement goals. If you are able to participate in a pension plan through your employer or union, it can be a good way to save for retirement and ensure a steady stream of income during your retirement years. However, you may also want to consider other retirement savings options, such as a 401(k) plan or an individual retirement account (IRA), to ensure that you have a diverse range of savings and investments for your retirement. It's important to carefully consider your options and consult with a financial professional to determine the best retirement savings strategy for your needs.

There are several retirement savings options available in Ireland, the UK, and Europe, including:

Occupational pension schemes: These are pension plans sponsored by an employer or union and are typically available to employees in certain industries or occupations. Occupational pension schemes can be either defined as benefit plans or defined contribution plans.

Personal pension plans: These are individual pension plans that individuals can set up on their own, without the sponsorship of an employer or union. Personal pension plans are typically defined contribution plans.

State pension schemes: In many countries, including Ireland, the UK, and several European countries, individuals may be entitled to receive a state pension upon reaching a certain age. The amount of the state pension is typically based on factors such as the individual's work history and contributions to the state pension system.

Individual retirement accounts (IRAs): These are tax-advantaged accounts that individuals can use to save for retirement. There are several different types of IRAs, including traditional IRAs and Roth IRAs.

401(k) plans: These are retirement savings plans that are sponsored by an employer and are available to employees in the United States. Employees contribute to their 401(k) account through payroll deductions, and the funds in the account grow tax-deferred until they are withdrawn at retirement.

It's important to carefully consider your options and consult with a financial professional to determine the best retirement savings strategy for your needs.

There are several factors to consider when determining if a financial professional is a good one:

Qualifications and credentials: Look for financial professionals who have the appropriate qualifications and credentials for the services they are offering. This may include a degree in a relevant field, such as finance or economics, as well as professional certifications, such as the Chartered Financial Analyst (CFA) or Certified Financial Planner (CFP) designation.

Experience: Consider the financial professional's level of experience in the industry and in providing the specific services you are seeking. A financial professional with more experience may have a better understanding of the market and be able to provide more informed guidance.

Fees: Understand how the financial professional charges for their services. Some financial professionals charge fees based on a percentage of the assets they manage, while others charge hourly or flat fees. Be sure to ask about the financial professional's fees upfront to ensure that you understand the cost of their services.

Professionalism: Look for financial professionals who are professional, ethical, and transparent in their dealings with clients. A financial professional who is willing to answer your questions and provide clear explanations of their recommendations is more likely to be trustworthy and competent.

Client testimonials: Consider the experiences of other clients who have worked with the financial professional. You may be able to find client testimonials on the financial professional's website or by asking for references.

It's also a good idea to do your own research and comparison-shopping to ensure that you are working with the best financial professional for your needs.

BUYING PROPERTY

There are several things to consider before applying for a mortgage when buying a property:

Your budget: Determine how much you can afford to borrow and what your monthly mortgage payments will be.

Your credit score: A good credit score will help you qualify for a better mortgage rate.

Your down payment: The more you can put down as a down payment, the lower your mortgage payments will be.

Your employment and income: Lenders will want to see that you have a stable income and employment history.

Your debts and liabilities: Lenders will consider your debts and liabilities when determining how much you can borrow.

The type of mortgage: There are different types of mortgages, such as fixed-rate and adjustable-rate mortgages. Consider which type is best for your situation.

The terms of the mortgage: Consider the length of the mortgage term, the interest rate, and any fees or closing costs associated with the loan.

Pre-approval: It's a good idea to get pre-approved for a mortgage before you start looking for a home. This will give you a good idea of how much you can borrow and what your monthly payments will be.

Shopping around: Don't just go with the first mortgage lender you find. Shop around and compare offers from multiple lenders to get the best deal.

You will need to choose between fixed and variable rate mortgages. It's not necessarily a question of one being "better" than the other, as both fixed-rate and adjustable-rate mortgages (ARMs) have their own advantages and disadvantages. It's important to consider your personal financial situation and goals when deciding which type of mortgage is right for you. Here are some things to consider when deciding between a fixed-rate and a variable-rate mortgage:

Fixed-rate mortgages:

· Interest rate remains the same throughout the term of the mortgage.

· Monthly payments are predictable and stable.

· May have a higher interest rate than a variable-rate mortgage.

Variable-rate mortgages:

· The interest rate can fluctuate over the term of the mortgage.

· May have a lower interest rate than a fixed-rate mortgage initially, but it could increase over time.

· Monthly payments may be less predictable.

If you prefer the stability and predictability of fixed monthly payments, a fixed-rate mortgage may be a good choice for you. On the other hand, if you are comfortable with the potential for fluctuating monthly payments and are willing to take on the risk of potentially higher interest rates in the future, a variable-rate mortgage may be a good option. Ultimately, the best choice for you will depend on your financial situation and your risk tolerance.

Your credit score

A credit score is a numerical representation of your creditworthiness, based on information in your credit report. Credit scores are typically used by lenders, landlords, and other creditors to evaluate your ability to pay back loans or debts. A higher credit score typically indicates a lower risk to the creditor, which may make you more likely to be approved for a loan or credit card, or to receive a lower interest rate on the loan.

Credit scores range from 300 to 850, with higher scores being considered better. Scores are calculated based on various factors in your credit report, including your payment history, the amount of debt you have, the length of your credit history, and the types of credit you have used.

Your credit score is important because it can affect your ability to borrow money and the terms you are offered. It's a good idea to check your credit score regularly and to work to improve it by paying bills on time, keeping your credit card balances low, and avoiding applying for new credit unnecessarily.

There are several options to consider to pay off your mortgage faster:

Make biweekly payments: Instead of making one monthly payment, you can make half a payment every two weeks. This can help you pay off your mortgage faster because you'll be making 26 half-payments per year, which is the equivalent of 13 full payments.

Make extra payments: If you have extra money available, you can make additional payments towards your mortgage principal. This will help reduce the balance of your loan and pay it off faster.

Refinance to a shorter term: If you have a long-term mortgage, such as a 30-year loan, you can refinance to a shorter term, such as a 15-year loan. This will increase your monthly payments, but you'll pay off the loan faster and may save money on interest in the long run.

Consider a mortgage acceleration program: Some lenders offer programs that allow you to pay extra towards your mortgage each month and apply the extra payments directly to your principal. This can help you pay off your mortgage faster.

Make a lump sum payment: If you have a large sum of money available, such as from a bonus or inheritance, you can make a lump sum payment towards your mortgage principal. This will reduce the balance of your loan and help you pay it off faster.

It's important to carefully consider the pros and cons of each option and to speak with a financial advisor or mortgage lender before making any decisions.

WILL CONSIDERATIONS

A will is a legal document that outlines how a person's property and assets should be distributed after their death. It also names an executor who is responsible for carrying out the terms of the will and a guardian for any minor children. A will allows a person to have control over what happens to their property and dependents after their death, rather than having the state make these decisions through the probate process. It is important to note that a will only becomes effective after a person dies and must be probated in court before it can be carried out. It is also important to review and update a will periodically to ensure that it reflects a person's current wishes and circumstances.

There are several types of wills that a person can choose from, depending on their circumstances and needs. Some common types of wills include:

Simple Will: A simple will is a basic document that outlines how a person's assets should be distributed after their death. It may also include provisions for the care of minor children and the appointment of an executor.

Testamentary Trust Will: A testamentary trust will is a type of will that includes provisions for the creation of a trust after the will-maker's death. This type of will allows the will-maker to specify how their assets should be managed and distributed after their death.

Living Will: A living will, also known as an advance directive, is a legal document that outlines a person's wishes for end-of-life medical care in the event that they become incapacitated and are unable to make decisions for themselves.

Pour-Over Will: A pour-over will is a type of will that is used in conjunction with a revocable living trust. It directs that any assets that are not transferred into the trust during the will maker's lifetime will be transferred into the trust after their death.

Mutual Will: A mutual will is a type of will that is made by two or more people, often a married couple, in which they agree to leave their property to each other or to specified beneficiaries.

It is important to consult with an attorney to determine which type of will is most appropriate for a person's individual needs and circumstances.

It is generally a good idea to review and update a will periodically to ensure that it reflects a person's current wishes and circumstances. Some common events that may prompt a person to update their will include:

Marriage or divorce: A person's will should be updated after they get married or divorced, as these events can significantly affect how their assets are distributed.

Birth or adoption of a child: If a person has a child after creating their will, they may want to update their will to provide for the care of their child in the event of their death.

Changes in assets or beneficiaries: If a person acquires or disposes of significant assets, or if their intended beneficiaries change, they may want to update their will to reflect these changes.

Changes in laws: Laws governing wills and estate planning can change over time, so it is a good idea to review a will periodically to ensure that it is still in compliance with current laws.

It is generally recommended to review a will at every few years, or sooner if any of the above events occur. It is also a good idea to review a will if a person moves to a new state, as different states have different laws governing wills and estate planning.

An executor is a person who is responsible for carrying out the instructions and provisions of a will after the person who made the will, the "testator", dies. The testator can appoint an executor in their will by naming them and describing their duties. The executor can be a family member, friend, professional (e.g. a lawyer or accountant), or an institution (e.g. a bank).

If the testator does not appoint an executor in their will, or if the person appointed is unable or unwilling to serve, the probate court may appoint an administrator to handle the estate. The administrator is typically a close relative of the deceased or a professional.

It's important to choose an executor carefully, as they will have significant responsibilities in managing the deceased's assets, paying debts and taxes, and distributing assets to beneficiaries. The executor should be someone who is organized, responsible, and able to handle the administrative tasks involved in settling an estate. It may also be a good idea to name a backup executor in case the primary executor is unable to serve.

The specific responsibilities of an executor will depend on the size and complexity of the estate and the laws of the state where the testator lived. In general, the executor's responsibilities may include:

Gathering and inventorying the deceased's assets: This includes identifying and locating all of the deceased's assets, such as bank accounts, investments, real estate, and personal property. The executor will also need to determine the value of these assets.

Paying debts and taxes: The executor will need to pay any outstanding debts and taxes that the deceased owed at the time of their death. This may include credit card bills, mortgages, and taxes owed to the government.

Distributing assets to beneficiaries: The executor will need to distribute the assets of the estate to the beneficiaries named in the will. This may include transferring ownership of assets to the beneficiaries, such as real estate or investments.

Filing the will and opening a probate case: In most states, the executor will need to file the will with the probate court and open a probate case. This will allow the court to oversee the administration of the estate and ensure that the will is carried out according to the testator's wishes.

Keeping records and reporting to the court: The executor will need to keep detailed records of all financial transactions related to the estate, and will need to report to the court on the progress of the estate administration.

In addition to these tasks, the executor may also need to deal with other matters related to the estate, such as selling assets, transferring titles, and obtaining appraisals. It's important for the executor to be organised and able to handle these tasks efficiently, as they can be time-consuming and complex.

INVENTORY CONSIDERATIONS

There are several steps that an executor can take to gather and inventory the assets of an estate:

Search for the will: The first step is to locate the will, as this document will outline the testator's wishes and may list some of the assets that are part of the estate. The will should be filed with the probate court, and a copy should also be kept with the testator's important papers.

Identify assets: The executor will need to identify all of the assets that are part of the estate. This may include bank accounts, investments, real estate, and personal property. The executor should search for any documents that may be helpful in locating these assets, such as bank statements, investment account statements, and property deeds.

Locate assets: Once the assets have been identified, the executor will need to locate them. This may involve contacting banks and financial institutions to locate accounts, or contacting real estate agents to locate property.

Determine value: The executor will need to determine the value of the assets in the estate. This may involve getting appraisals for real estate, artwork, and other valuable items, or obtaining statements from banks and investment firms to determine the value of accounts.

Create an inventory: Once all of the assets have been located and valued, the executor should create an inventory of the assets in the estate. This inventory should include a description of each asset, its value, and any relevant documentation. The inventory will be used to help distribute the assets of the estate to the beneficiaries.

It's important for the executor to be thorough and accurate when gathering and inventorying the assets of the estate, as this will help to ensure that the will is carried out correctly and that all assets are accounted for.

Once the executor has completed all of their responsibilities, they will need to close the estate. This typically involves completing a final accounting of all financial transactions related to the estate and obtaining court approval for the distribution of assets to the beneficiaries. To close the estate, the executor will typically need to:

Prepare a final accounting: The executor should prepare a final accounting of all financial transactions related to the estate. This should include a list of all assets and debts, as well as a record of any income or expenses incurred during the estate administration.

File the final accounting with the court: The executor will need to file the final accounting with the probate court, along with any other necessary documents. The court will review the accounting to ensure that it is accurate and complete.

Obtain court approval: The executor will need to obtain court approval for the distribution of assets to the beneficiaries. This may involve appearing in court to present the final accounting and answer any questions the judge may have.

Distribute assets to beneficiaries: Once the court has approved the distribution of assets, the executor can distribute the assets to the beneficiaries according to the terms of the will.

File final papers: The executor will need to file any final papers with the court, such as a petition for discharge or a certificate of completion, to officially close the estate.

It's important for the executor to keep the beneficiaries informed throughout the process and to follow all legal requirements when closing the estate. This will help to ensure that the distribution of assets is carried out smoothly and that the beneficiaries receive their inheritances according to the testator's wishes.

There are several documents that a testator should have in order to facilitate the gathering and inventorying of their assets after their death:

Will: The most important document is the will itself, which outlines the testator's wishes and names the executor who will be responsible for carrying out those wishes. The will should be kept in a safe place and a copy should be provided to the executor.

Asset list: It may be helpful for the testator to create a list of their assets, including bank accounts, investments, real estate, and personal property. This list should include the name of each asset, its location, and any relevant account numbers or other identifying information.

Financial documents: The testator should keep important financial documents, such as bank statements, investment account statements, and tax returns, in a safe place. These documents will be useful in locating and valuing the testator's assets.

Property deeds: If the testator owns real estate, they should keep the deeds to their property in a safe place. These deeds will be necessary to transfer ownership of the property to the beneficiaries.

Other important papers: The testator should also keep any other important papers, such as insurance policies, contracts, and powers of attorney, in a safe place. These documents may be relevant to the administration of the estate.

By keeping these documents organized and easily accessible, the testator can make it easier for the executor to gather and inventory their assets after their death.

A power of attorney is a legal document that gives another person the authority to act on your behalf. The person who gives the power of attorney is called the "principal," and the person who receives the power of attorney is called the "agent" or "attorney-in-fact."

There are two main types of power of attorney:

Durable power of attorney: This type of power of attorney remains in effect even if the principal becomes incapacitated or unable to make decisions for themselves. This can be useful if the principal becomes incapacitated due to illness or injury and is unable to manage their own affairs.

Non-durable power of attorney: This type of power of attorney is only effective while the principal is capable of making their own decisions. It typically expires if the principal becomes incapacitated.

A power of attorney can be general, which gives the agent broad authority to make decisions and take actions on behalf of the principal, or it can be limited, which gives the agent only specific powers.

A power of attorney can be useful in a variety of situations, such as if the principal is going to be out of town and needs someone to handle their financial affairs while they are away, or if the principal becomes incapacitated and is unable to make decisions for themselves.

It's important to choose an agent carefully, as they will have significant authority to act on your behalf. It may also be a good idea to name a backup agent in case the primary agent is unable or unwilling to serve.

Sample of a power of attorney document:

"I, [Name], of [Address], hereby appoint [Name] of [Address] as my attorney-in-fact. I grant my attorney-in-fact full power and authority to act on my behalf in any and all legal matters, including but not limited to:

Managing my financial affairs

Buying, selling, and transferring property

Entering into contracts

Signing documents on my behalf

This power of attorney is effective immediately and shall remain in effect until I revoke it or until my death.

I declare under penalty of perjury that the foregoing is true and correct.

Signed,

[Name]. [Date]

Witnessed by:

[Name] [Date]"

This is just one example of a power of attorney document, and the specific language and provisions may vary depending on the state where it is executed and the specific needs and wishes of the principal. It's important to have a power of attorney document prepared by a lawyer to ensure that it is legally valid and meets all the necessary requirements.

Sample of a durable power of attorney document:

"I, [Name], of [Address], hereby appoint [Name] of [Address] as my attorney-in-fact. I grant my attorney-in-fact full power and authority to act on my behalf in any and all legal matters, including but not limited to:

Managing my financial affairs

Buying, selling, and transferring property

Entering into contracts

Signing documents on my behalf

This power of attorney shall not be affected by my subsequent incapacity.

I declare under penalty of perjury that the foregoing is true and correct.

Signed,

[Name] [Date]

Witnessed by:

[Name]. [Date]"

This is just one example of a durable power of attorney document, and the specific language and provisions may vary depending on the state where it is executed and the specific needs and wishes of the principal. It's important to have a durable power of attorney document prepared by a lawyer to ensure that it is legally valid and meets all the necessary requirements. A durable power of attorney can be a useful tool for ensuring that someone has the authority to manage your affairs if you become incapacitated and are unable to do so yourself.

REGULATIONS CONSIDERATIONS

The Brussels IV regulations are specific to the European Union (EU) and do not apply to countries outside the EU. However, many countries have similar rules and regulations that govern the choice of law and jurisdiction in matters of succession.

Brussels IV is a set of regulations that govern the choice of law and jurisdiction in matters of succession in the European Union (EU). These regulations aim to provide clarity and predictability in the determination of which country's laws apply to the succession of a deceased person's estate, and which courts have jurisdiction to hear disputes related to the succession.

The Brussels IV regulations apply to individuals who are citizens of EU member states and to the succession of their movable and immovable property located in the EU. The regulations also apply to the succession of property located outside the EU if the deceased person was a citizen of an EU member state at the time of their death.

The Brussels IV regulations provide for the possibility of choosing the law that will govern the succession of a deceased person's estate, as well as the jurisdiction of the courts that will hear any disputes related to the succession. The regulations also provide for the recognition and enforcement of judicial decisions made in other EU member states in relation to the succession of a deceased person's estate.

Overall, the Brussels IV regulations aim to provide a more streamlined and efficient process for the determination of the law and jurisdiction in matters of succession, helping to ensure that the rights of the deceased person's heirs are protected and that their estate is properly administered.

In the United States, for example, the choice of law and jurisdiction in matters of succession is governed by state law, as well as by federal laws such as the Uniform Probate Code (UPC). The UPC is a model law that has been adopted in some form by many states in the U.S., and it provides rules and procedures for the administration of estates and the distribution of a deceased person's property.

Similarly, other countries have their own laws and regulations that govern the choice of law and jurisdiction in matters of succession. These laws may be based on civil law principles, common law principles, or a combination of both. The specific laws and regulations that apply in a given country will depend on the legal system in place in that country.

PLEASE ENSURE YOU CONSULT PROFESSIONALS,
THIS IS AN EDUCATIONAL GUIDE ONLY.